Happiness

. . . it's as easy as . . .

A B C

This book is dedicated to my family.

To my Dad, Ralph Ames, who taught me to appreciate the power of words.

To my youngest sister Laura, who will always be an inspiration to me. Laura passed away in 2011.

And to my Mom, Carol, and my sisters – Judy, Chris, Kathy and Trish.

Sisters: (L to R) Kathy, Cindy, Chris, Judy, Laura, and Trish

Thank you so much for your loving support.

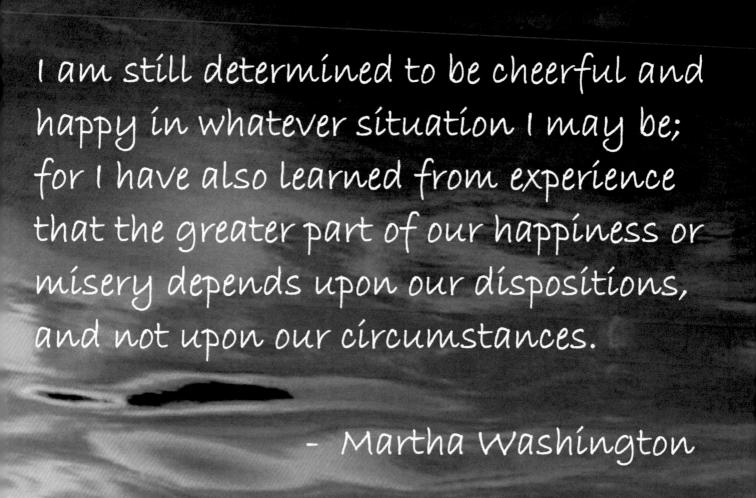

I am still determined to be cheerful and happy in whatever situation I may be; for I have also learned from experience that the greater part of our happiness or misery depends upon our dispositions, and not upon our circumstances.

- Martha Washington

Introduction

One afternoon, as I was vacationing in Hawaii, I became acutely aware of the dichotomy between the language people around me were using and their surroundings. I was walking past a street of shops overlooking the Pacific Ocean and I heard a sales associate welcoming customers into his store and asking each as they passed by him, "How are you doing?" Over and over I heard people respond with an obligatory "fine" or "OK" - and I was intrigued by the complacency of these answers.

We were not on a street, waiting for a bus, during a snow storm. We were in Hawaii - in February - and the sun was shining, the air was warm and clear, and the breeze off the ocean brought with it the intoxicating fragrance of exotic flowers. Were the people around here really just OK? Were they oblivious to the beautiful surroundings? Where would these people have to be, or what would they need to be doing, to provide a more positive and thoughtful response?

Ever since that day I have been more conscious of the words people choose to use to describe how they are feeling, what they are doing or what they intend to do. I created this book to help people understand how the words they use in their daily lives affect themselves and others around them.

Below are a few fun exercises that you can do to help find ways of incorporating better/more thoughtful/positive words into your vocabulary.

#1 - The Greeting Challenge

The next time someone asks you how you are doing, challenge yourself to come up with a different or even a positive response. Try: "I'm great." "My life is awesome." "Things couldn't be better." I must admit that, on some occasions, when I'm not feeling all that great, I have used the word "Unbelievable!" Although it's a rather ambiguous response, it's way better than "OK."

Make it a game. Have fun. Brainstorm some replies that would work for you. If you were to try this exercise for even one day, you would be amazed at the responses it will evoke.

#2 - What Is Your Password?

Do you spend much time at a computer? How many times a day are you entering your password? When selecting a new password, use a positive word such as Fabulous or Fantastic. Every time you enter that new password you will be reminded of the good things in your life.

#3 - The Alphabet Game

Ask yourself the following question: "What positive qualities do I possess or do I want to incorporate into my life?" Then, answer that question with words that begin with the letter A, then B, and C. Run through the whole alphabet and come up with one or more words that begin with each letter.

Sounds easy right? Take a walk and try it. The feedback I have received from others trying this exercise is that it is much harder than they thought it would be.

Most tell me that the first words that came to mind for each letter were almost always negative (i.e., A is for Awful, B is for Bad). Some have said that it either took a really long time or they couldn't think of a single positive quality beginning with any letter - thus the reason for this book.

Take time to consider "A is for Amazing" and "B is for Brave and Brilliant" and "C is for Compassionate and Curious and Creative." This exercise will work for every letter in the alphabet except the letter X. To solve this dilemma simply replace X with the prefix EX. Thank goodness for phonics.

Perhaps this exercise is initially difficult because so much of our lives are consumed with negative thoughts, feelings and input. Or perhaps it's just that we don't spend much time focusing on the positive aspects of daily life. Do performance appraisals focus on what you do well and the raise you deserve, or on what you need to improve upon before you are entitled to that raise? When you take a test, do you focus on how many of your answers were right, or how many were incorrect? When people you know seek to engage in conversation, do they most often ask, "What's going right in your life?" or are they more likely to ask, "What's wrong?"

The concept behind each of these exercises is to get you to experience how the use of positive/more thoughtful words can affect your life. The more you repeat each exercise, the better you will become.

Here's to your best life!   Enjoy!

A

Adventurous

Affluent

Amazing

Ambitious

Appealing

Appreciative

Articulate

Attentive

Attractive

Authentic

Awesome

_____

_____

_____

It is our attitude at the beginning of a difficult task which, more than anything else, will affect its successful outcome.

- William James

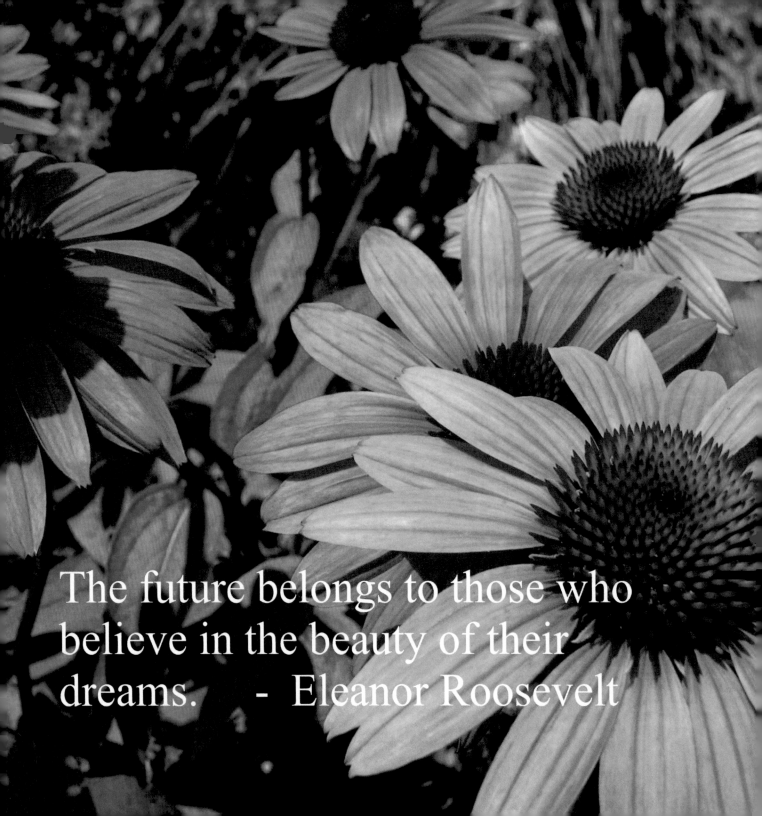

The future belongs to those who believe in the beauty of their dreams.   - Eleanor Roosevelt

B

Balanced
Beautiful
Believable
Benevolent
Blessed
Bold

Brave
Bright
Brilliant

_____

_____

_____

C

Captivating Courageous
Caring   Creative
Charming   Credible
Cheerful   Curious
Clever
Confident   _____
            _____

If you don't like something, change it; if you can't change it, change the way you think about it.
- Mary Engelbreit

D

Daring
Dazzling
Decisive
Dedicated
Delightful
Deserving
Determined

Devoted
Disciplined
Divine
Dynamic

_____
_____
_____

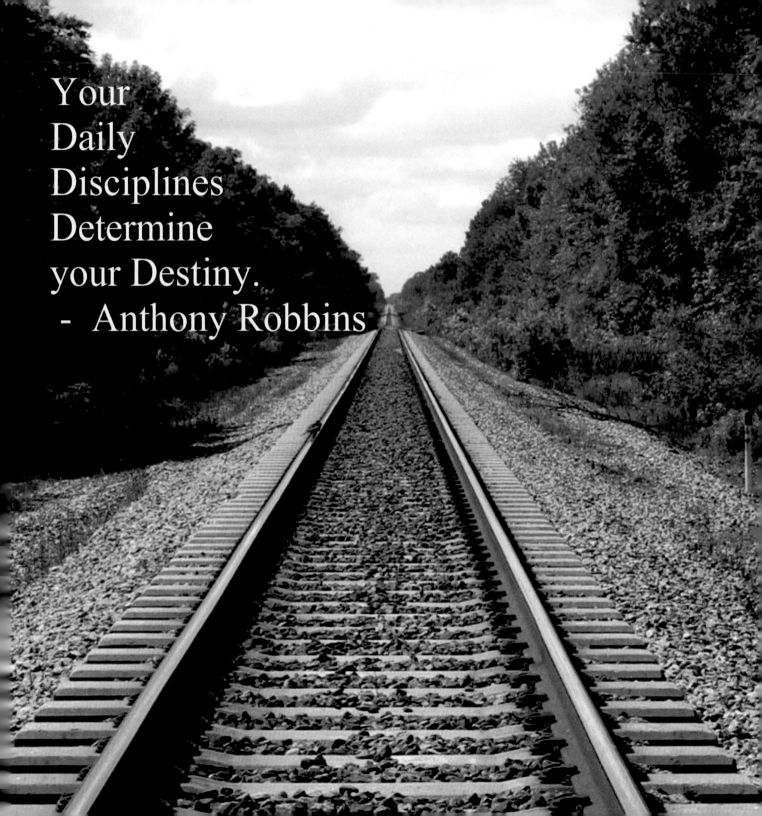

Your
Daily
Disciplines
Determine
your Destiny.
 - Anthony Robbins

E

Eager
Effervescent
Eligible
Enchanting
Encouraging

Energetic
Enthusiastic

_____

_____

_____

We act as though comfort and luxury were the chief requirements of life, when all that we need to make us really happy is something to be enthusiastic about.
- Charles Kingsley

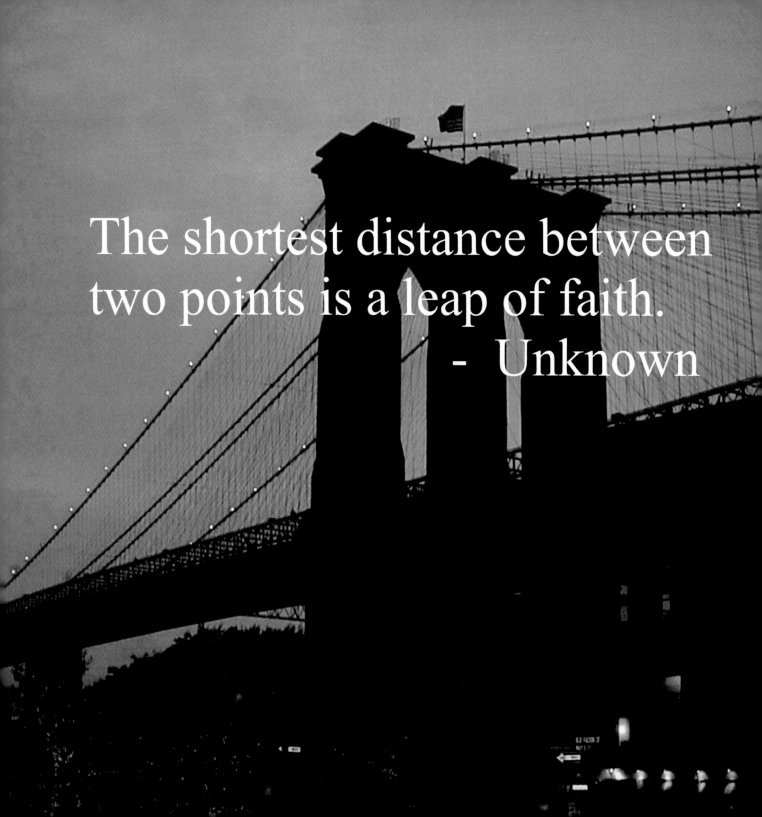

The shortest distance between two points is a leap of faith.
- Unknown

F

Fabulous	Free
Faithful	Friendly
Fantastic	Fulfilled
Fearless	Fun
Flexible	_____
Focused	_____
Fortunate	_____

G

Generous

Gentle

Giving

Good

Graceful

Gracious

Grateful

Great

Guided

_____

_____

_____

Let your hopes, not your hurts,
shape your future.
                    - Robert H. Schuller

H

Handsome   Humble

Happy   Humorous

Healthy

Helpful   _____

Honorable   _____

_____

If you can recognize the need
for improvement, things are
already improving.
- Unknown

I

Ideal	Intelligent
Imaginative	Intense
Incredible	Inventive
Independent	Invincible
Insightful	_____
Inspiring	_____

J

Jolly

Joyful

Jubilant

Just

_____

_____

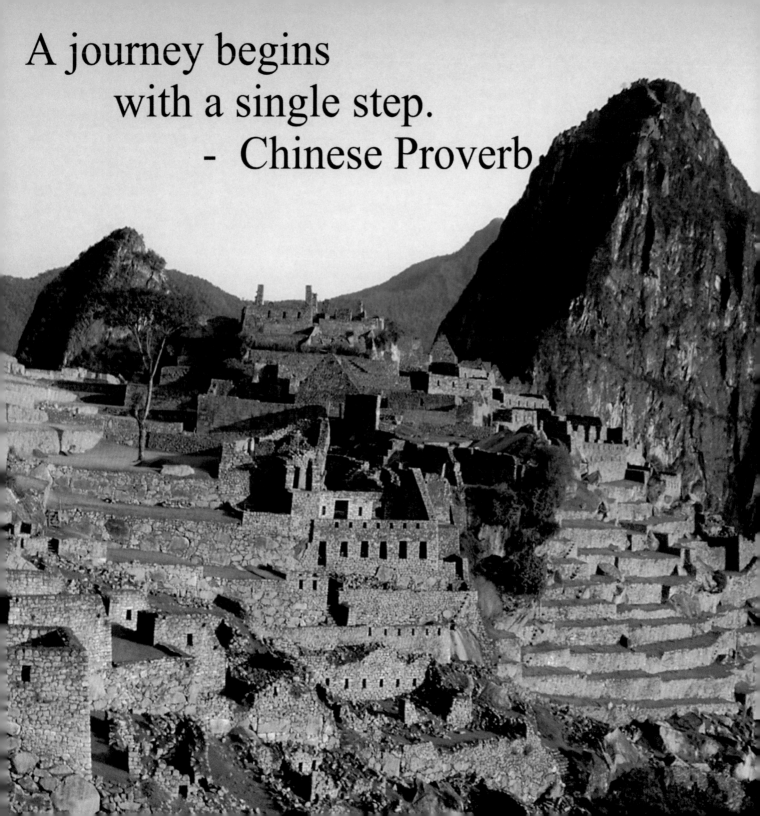

A journey begins
    with a single step.
        - Chinese Proverb

Three things in human life are important. The first is to be kind. The second is to be kind. And the third is to be kind.
- Henry James

K

Kind
Knowledgeable

_____

_____

L

Legendary   Lucid

Liberated   Lucky

Lively

Lovely   _____

Loving   _____

                     _____

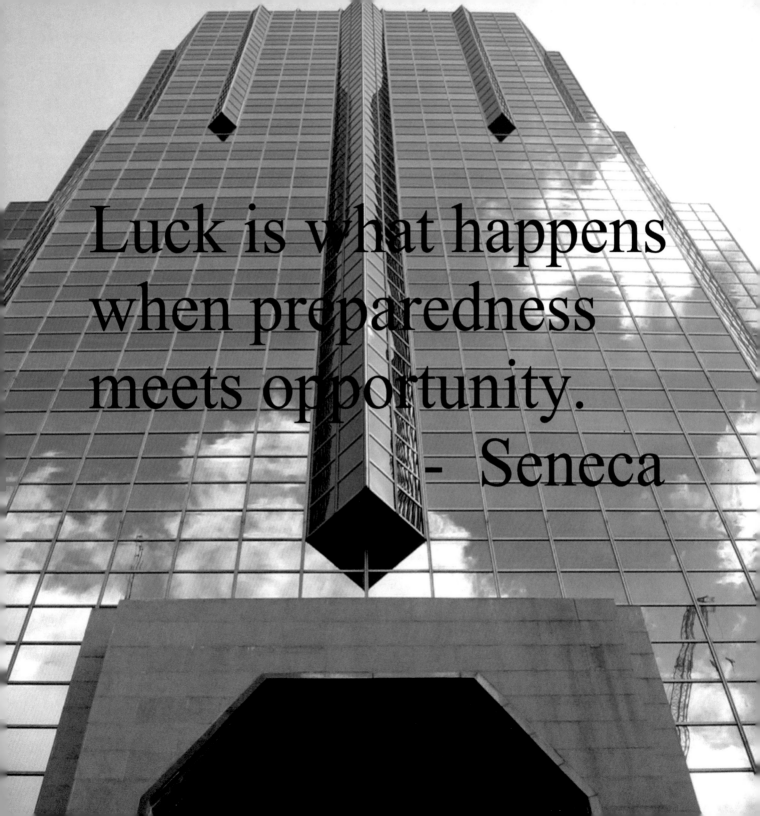

Luck is what happens when preparedness meets opportunity.
        - Seneca

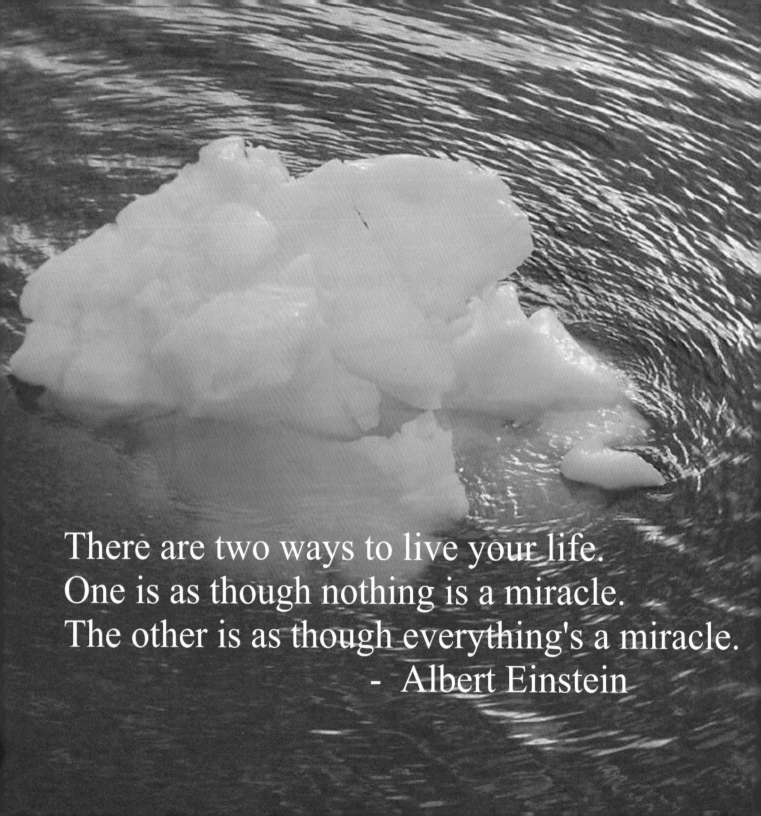

There are two ways to live your life.
One is as though nothing is a miracle.
The other is as though everything's a miracle.
- Albert Einstein

M

Magical

Magnificent

Marvelous

Masterful

Merry

Mesmerizing

Mighty

Motivated

Mysterious

_____

_____

_____

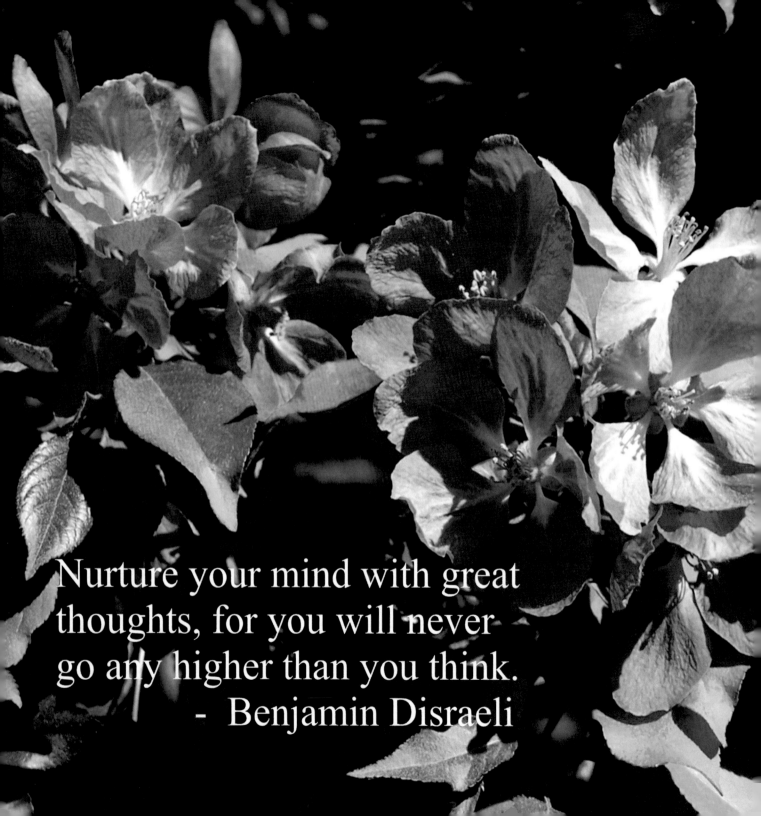

Nurture your mind with great
thoughts, for you will never
go any higher than you think.
        - Benjamin Disraeli

N

Neat

Necessary

Nice

Noble

Nurturing

_____

_____

_____

O

Observant   Outrageous

Open   Outstanding

Optimistic   _____

Organized   _____

A pessimist sees difficulty in every opportunity; An optimist sees the opportunity in every difficulty.

- Sir Winston Churchill

P

Passionate

Patient

Peaceful

Perceptive

Phenomenal

Playful

Pleasant

Positive

Powerful

Prepared

Profound

Prosperous

Proud

Punctual

_____

_____

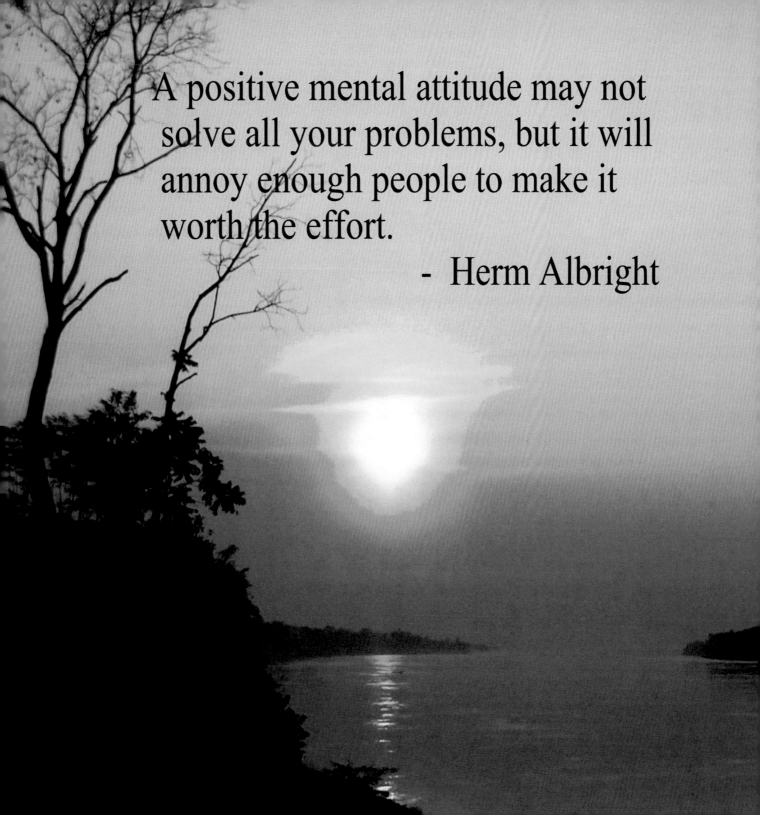

A positive mental attitude may not solve all your problems, but it will annoy enough people to make it worth the effort.

- Herm Albright

A quiet mind is the foundation of inner peace.
And inner peace translates into outer peace.
                                        - Unknown

Q

Qualified
Quiet
Quick
Quotable

_____

_____

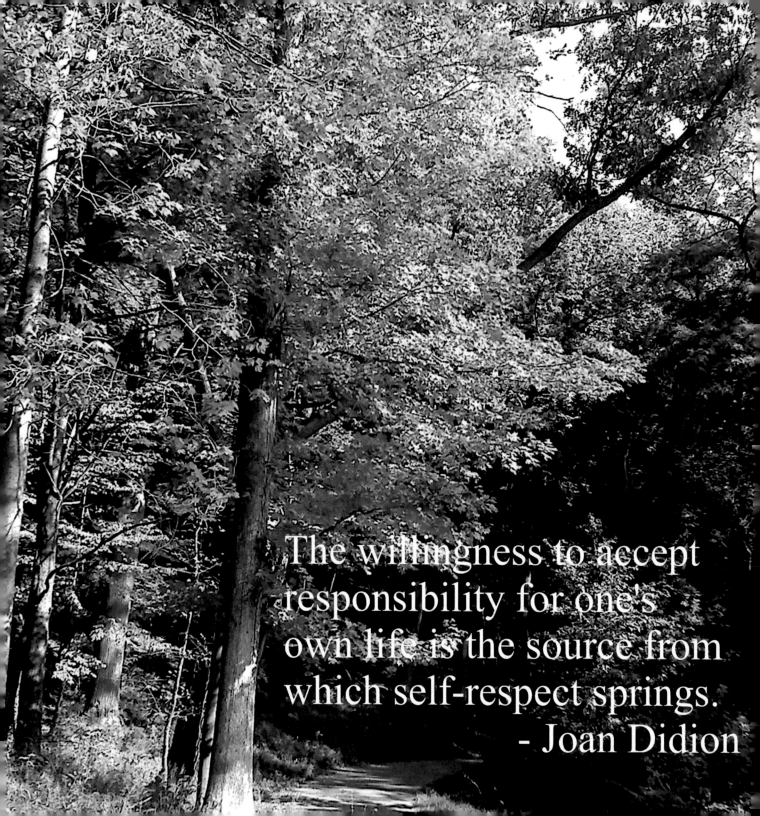

The willingness to accept
responsibility for one's
own life is the source from
which self-respect springs.
    - Joan Didion

R

Radiant

Relevant

Remarkable

Resilient

Resourceful

Respectful

Responsive

Responsible

Rich

_____

_____

_____

S

Secure
Sensational
Skillful
Smart
Sparkling
Spectacular

Stimulating
Strong
Successful

_____
_____
_____

Before anything else,
getting ready is the
secret to success.
 - Henry Ford

T

Talented Transformed
Terrific Tremendous
Thankful Triumphant
Thoughtful Trustworthy
Thriving Truthful
Thrilled _____
Tranquil _____

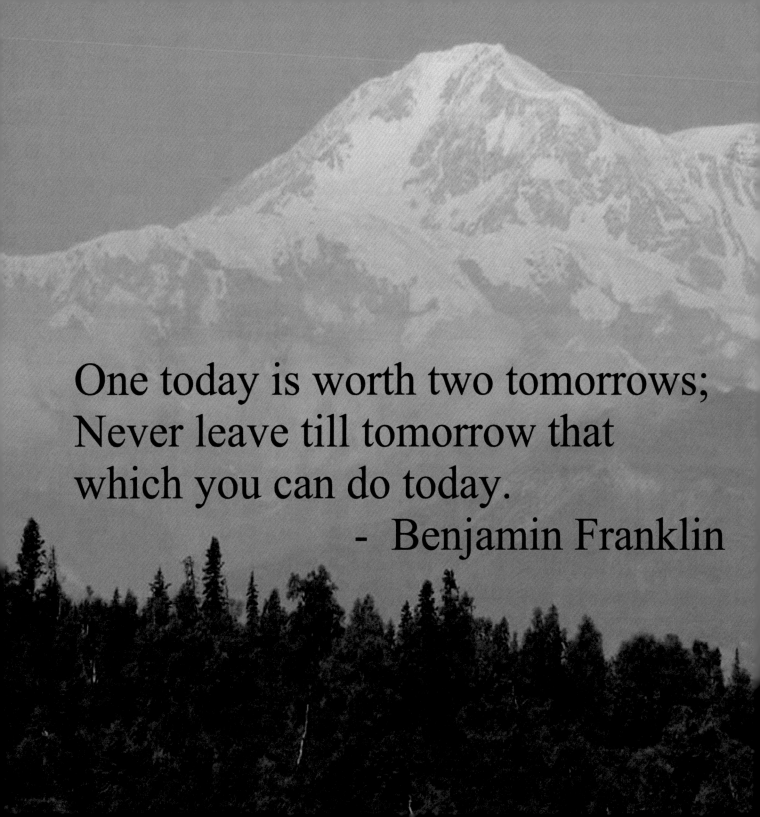

One today is worth two tomorrows;
Never leave till tomorrow that
which you can do today.

- Benjamin Franklin

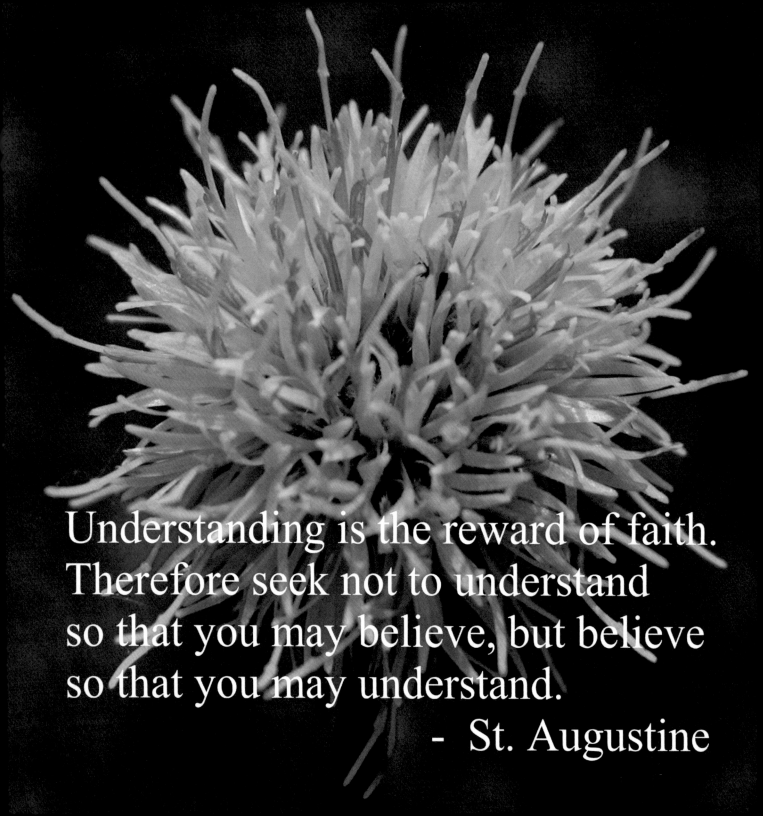

Understanding is the reward of faith. Therefore seek not to understand so that you may believe, but believe so that you may understand.

- St. Augustine

U

Understanding
Unforgettable
Unique
Uplifting
Useful

_____

_____

V

Valiant

Valuable

Versatile

Vibrant

Victorious

Vigilant

Vigorous

Vital

Vivacious

_____

_____

_____

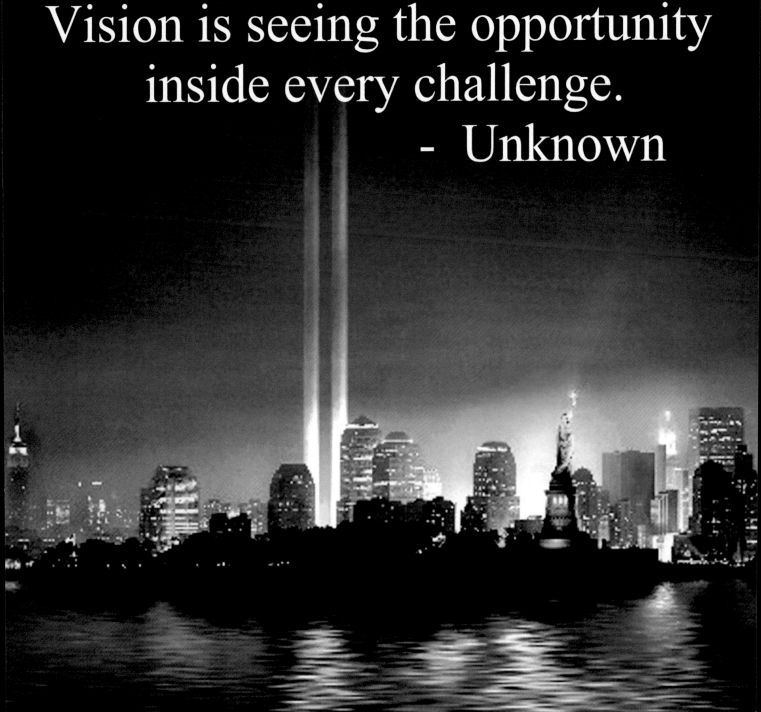

Vision is seeing the opportunity inside every challenge.
- Unknown

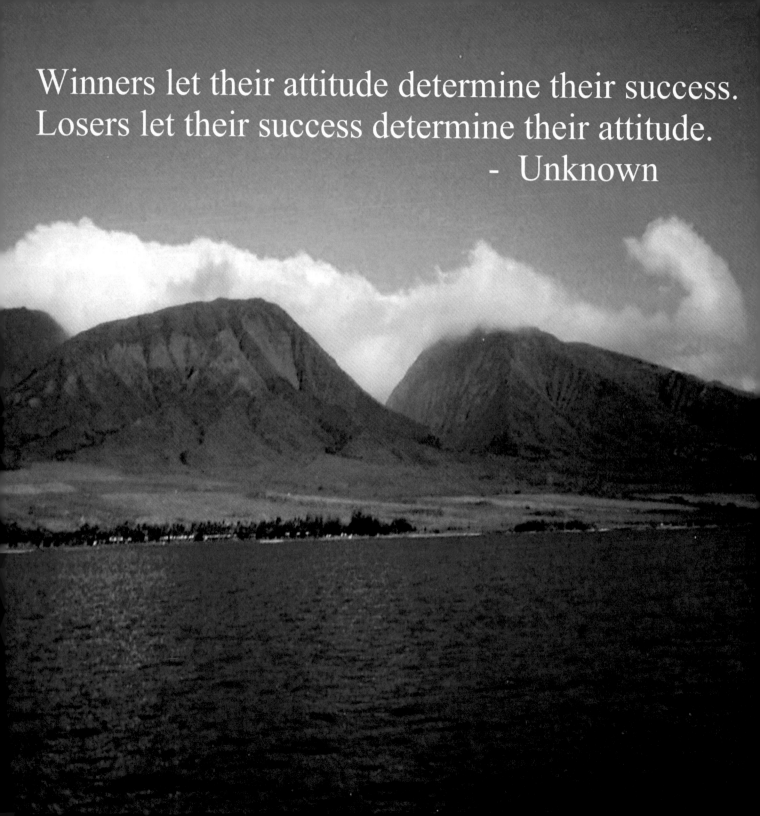

Winners let their attitude determine their success.
Losers let their success determine their attitude.
- Unknown

W

Warm   Witty
Wealthy   Wonderful
Welcoming   Worthy
Whimsical
Willing   _____
Wise   _____
             _____

E+X

Excellent   Experienced

Exceptional   Expressive

Excited   Exuberant

Exemplary   _____

Exhilarated   _____

We are what we repeatedly do.
Excellence, then, is not
an act but a habit.

- Aristotle

It only takes one person to change your life

- YOU.

- Ruth Casey

Y

Yearning
Yielding
Young
Youthful

_____

_____

Z

Zany
Zealous
Zesty
Zippy

_____

_____

The only Zen you find on the
tops of mountains is the Zen
you bring up there.
      - Robert Pirsig

Photo Credits

Front Cover & Cover Page – Laura Ames Acord

Page:

3: Kezar Lake – Cindy Ames

9: Clouds at Honeoye Lake – Cindy Ames

10: Flowers – Laura Ames Acord

13: Genesee River – Cindy Ames

15: Railroad Tracks – Laura Ames Acord

17: Yellow Flower – Laura Ames Acord

18: Brooklyn Bridge – Laura Ames Acord

20: Ellison Park – Cindy Ames

22: Peruvian Flower – Cindy Ames

24: Erie Canal – Cindy Ames

27: Machu Pichu – Cindy Ames

28: Hand – Laura Ames Acord

31: Skyscraper – Laura Ames Acord

32: Alaskan Iceberg – Cindy Ames

Page:

34: Apple Blossoms – Cindy Ames

37: Red Barn – Laura Ames Acord

39: Sunrise on the Amazon – Cindy Ames

40: Overpass – Laura Ames Acord

42: Fall Foliage – Cindy Ames

45: Carnival Ride – Laura Ames Acord

47: Mt. McKinley – Cindy Ames

48: Exotic Flower – Laura Ames Acord

51: NYC Skyline – Laura Ames Acord

52: Hawaii – Cindy Ames

55: Spring Bouquet – Laura Ames Acord

56: Alaskan Glacier – Cindy Ames

59: Valley of Fire – Cindy Ames

60: Beach in Lima – Cindy Ames

Made in the USA
San Bernardino, CA
25 January 2018